SIGNS WONDERS AND MIRACLES

Testimonies from The Summit
Volume 1

ISBN: 9798403380737

Published by Summit Global Publishing Ltd. on February 11, 2022

8717 50 St NW, Edmonton, AB, T6B1E7
info@summitglobalpublishing.com

Compiled by Tracy Belford

Edited by Ruth Wadley, Barbara Bearht, Tracy Belford

Cover by Krysta Koppel

Scripture quotations marked NLT are taken from the *Holy Bible*, New Living Translation, Copyright © 1996, 2004, 2015 by Tyndale House Foundation. Used by permission of Tyndale House Publishers, Inc., Carol Stream, Illinois 60188. All rights reserved.

Contents

"For ever since the world was created, people have seen the earth and sky. Through everything God made, they can clearly see his invisible qualities— his eternal power and divine nature. So they have no excuse for not knowing God." Romans 1:20 NLT

Introduction

God is supreme over the laws of nature. This means that every now and then, He chooses to lay aside the normal rules of the universe and do something miraculous. As Christians we are instructed to do what Jesus did. When Jesus walked the earth, He performed signs, wonders, miracles, and healings everywhere He went. That means that those things should follow us where we go too!

"These miraculous signs will accompany those who believe: They will cast out demons in my name, and they will speak in new languages. They will be able to handle snakes with safety, and if they drink anything poisonous, it won't hurt them. They will be able to place their hands on the sick, and they will be healed." Mark 16:17-18 NLT

This book is all about the stories of things God has done that are out of the ordinary and special. They are signs, miracles, and wonders. These are just a small fraction of the miracles God has done at The Summit Edmonton Church this year. There were many, many more that we have not recorded.

These stories have been written down to encourage you and to show God's glory. We don't want to give credit to ourselves because they are truly all God's hand and His design, so our part in these miracles is really only about our obedience. We are not somehow different than the average believer. YOU too can see God work miracles. All that is required is faith and obedience. So go ahead, pray for that sick person. Call on God for a financial miracle. Ask Him to do something wild and crazy and watch Him come through in ways you never dreamed of!

If you have a testimony you'd like to share with us to be included in our next collection, email tracy@thesummitchurch.ca.

Tracy Belford

Summit Global Publishing Ltd.

Testimonies About a Change of Heart

I met Pastor T.J. 5 years ago when I heard him speak about revival. I caught him after the service and hammered him with questions, and his answers began to show me that 'revival' was more than just meetings where the leaders of the church get exhausted and the moms or dads at home get stressed and tired of parenting alone. That conversation began a process of healing pain in my life that I didn't even know was there. When I got home that night, I told my husband, "You gotta meet this guy. There's just something about him, that I know one day we will be connected in some way."

Fast forward 4.5 years to last summer, when we began to feel God shifting us out of everything we knew. We pushed back a little; it's not easy to move a family like ours out of the church we grew up in, and raised our kids in. By the end of October last year, we had stepped down from where I had spent the last 21 years and moved our family to the Summit West location.

It wasn't always easy, moving brought challenges. Those challenges were always met with grace and love, and many helping hands from the family we found here. In the following months, God took us on a journey, week after week, of learning that He wants us to just 'be' instead of 'do'. Personally, I spent the last decade unintentionally focusing on 'doing' and had lost sight of my identity as a daughter of God.

I told a friend of mine that I felt like clay on the potter's wheel, but I figured that what I had built was quite beautiful, even though my heart knew that God needed to be the builder, not me. I told her that as the clay, I wanted to jump off the wheel and hide before it all got smushed down. But I didn't. Instead, I learned to trust.

Through the last 7 months, God has done a lot of excavation in our hearts. We have been in a season of rest, which is an altogether new and somewhat uncomfortable thing for me. I'm learning that rest doesn't just mean not doing anything, it's a posture of the heart, being confident in my identity as a daughter of God, aside from anything that I might 'do.'

We have also seen our family grow closer together and our kids are hearing from God more than ever. We have had powerful conversations with them and have seen growth in many areas. We are so thankful for the relationships we've begun to find here - mothers, fathers, sisters, and brothers. We absolutely look forward to being a part of what God is doing at The Summit West location.

Beki Ryzuk, May 2021

I had many years in my adult life where I was trying to live life my way and I believed a lot of twisted theologies about my purpose in life. It wasn't until about age 30 (I'm 36 now) that my wife and I were being encouraged to re-enter a church environment by our young boy. At that time, Holy Spirit led me to repentance and then transformation.

The next years were amazing because God was freeing me and many of my priorities were drastically shifting. I became a much better husband and father than I could ever be on my own.

We had some amazing and beautiful people mentor us throughout the years too. The Summit Edmonton Church (who we originally met through tent meetings held in the Cold Lake area) is included in that list and taught us that worship can be fun, freeing, and passionate.

What God is showing me is that He is really big, and we really are in no place to assume we understand all of Him. In fact, I've learned that if we assume God interacts with all of us the same way, we're bound to hurt other people. Something that one person finds encouraging might actually make another person feel like they're not Christian enough and will never measure up.

The night before my last trip to The Summit in Edmonton, I told God "I'm ok if you single me out tomorrow, if you have a word for me." I was still a little surprised when Pastor TJ gave me one. I thank TJ for his obedience because I know without any doubt that it was from God.

TJ spoke of a hope in God that I held onto. It was referring to the fact that I still know God is genuine and He is most definitely good despite the messiness of the church body. To know that God has these kinds of plans for me and my family is extremely encouraging. The word TJ gave me was about wisdom and an anointing for business that I will receive in the coming years; in addition, that God will restore to me resources that I have lost.

Adam Pequegnat, July 2021

My husband and I were leaving for our first trip away since COVID started, and I was quite nervous. We were at the airport checking in. I almost ran out of the check-in desk from panic, and I thought to myself (and God) "It would make me feel better if we see someone we know." And who does God bring across our path, but an intercessor from our church, also on her way to fly somewhere! God is faithful, even in these things.

Destiny Plante, August 2021

I received a breakthrough. Actually, that's not the right word. A clarification that brought healing. We had a Leader's Training at church. It started with worship and during that time I was hit with a deep grief because of pain in regard to feeling like I've never been pursued. That's how I've felt for a very long time. I spent 18 years with a man who deliberately withheld affection and intimacy. It's an accumulative pain that is hard to describe. To survive that, I developed some skills that protected my heart and soul, but that came with side effects. Holy Spirit gave me the tools that were needed in that time, however they are no longer required.

At the Leader's Training, I was on the floor bawling and purging my pain. It was raw and I knew it was incomplete. I had a knowing that the healing would continue. The next day, I walked into the sanctuary, and I felt God's presence instantly. At pre-service prayer, I was on my knees asking for Him to expose what needed to be exposed and heal the reasons why I felt this way.

I 'know' in my head that I'm loved by many. But I don't really feel it. There's a wall of protection that I needed to survive, but that wall also seemed to keep some of the good out too.

I was soaking, crying, and worshiping and the root appeared before me. It was a moment when I was twelve years old. Puberty was very fast for me, my body changed overnight. Throughout my childhood my dad would say our prayers and give us a back rub before bed. It was one of my favourite things. But after my body changed, he told me one day that he couldn't do that anymore for me. I know that for him it was what he needed to do, but for a girl who was still a child, it created a hole and a need that I attempted to fill with many boyfriends over the next couple years. I've spent my life waiting for love, romance, and connection. I've also had a lot of love in my life too, don't get me wrong. But in this specific area there's been a deficit.

Back to the point. After the picture of that moment with my dad, it became clear to me that it wasn't actually about being pursued or loved at all. The root was that seed of rejection. Honestly, I haven't thought about that moment in decades. It's not something that's ever in my mind. The Holy Spirit fascinates me when He does that.

Now with a point to deal with, I spent the rest of worship working through that revelation. When I can name something, I am able to quickly deal with it in my heart and mind. That day was so cleansing. I feel like a deep wound is now on the way to wholeness. I feel like walls are being dismantled. They were put up for a reason and purpose over the years, but they are no longer needed. That weekend was a divine encounter with peace.

Ruth W, November 2021

I've been under a spirit of rebellion for a long time, and it became a part of my identity. But on December 4, 2021, at the True North Revival night, I asked my mom to pray it off me. She helped me to rebuke it and I asked the Holy Spirit to fill that part of my heart so that my identity would be one who loves God and shows it through obedience.

My value and identity is not in being different.

Glory Belford, December 2021

There was a guy that had been coming to the Summit. He reached out for some help. I called him up and we met at Tim Horton's. I knew he had kind of a sensitive story and I said, "Let's go back to the parking lot by my truck. We'll have coffee on the tailgate." We were sitting there, and it was pretty busy. We started talking about the things of God. I began showing him love by praying for him and giving Him Jesus, and he started to bawl right there in the parking lot, as God touched his heart.

Des Belford, August 2021

I attended the East location at the 11:30 service and I loved the worship; it was so powerful. I've always loved worship since I was a kid. I attended church with my nanny, but I was lost. I lost my way with drugs. I'm in the process of becoming who I am meant to be and forming a better relationship with my Creator. Thank you for welcoming me and I'm excited to have my boyfriend join as well. Together, we can finally live a Christian life like we've always talked about.

Anonymous, August 2021

Someone I prayed for yesterday texted me and she said, "My whole world shifted after yesterday. The breakthrough I have been pressing in for since January happened. I want to thank you for allowing me to just sob in your arms as Holy Spirit ministered through you deep into my heart."

Tracy Belford, November 2021

I showed my kids a video of the end part of a True North service, and Isaiah, who is 7, was so moved. He said, "I need to be there next time!" He was sitting next to me grooving and worshipping as he watched the video. Then he said, "Mom, we need to be there early, and we need to get to the front, and I need to be up at the front worshiping." Without my prompting, he has been caught up in moments of worship. It's been beautiful to watch.

Krysta Koppel, November 2021

Warning the following testimony contains mature content.

I grew up in a Christian home. My mom was so in love with God. He literally saved her life and my eldest sister's, which is what brought her to God in the first place. My youngest childhood memory was coming home from church in our Sunday dresses on a warm summer day. I remember my mom was always praying and trying to teach us about God. She was so caring and loving; her heart was so pure. She dedicated her life to helping others, preaching, singing and volunteering all her extra time to the Hope Mission. She wasn't scared to tell others about God or to burst out in songs. Almost every night, she would come into our rooms with her guitar and sing us Christian songs. We prayed for every meal, we had Bible studies at home, we went to church every Sunday, we went to Bible camps, youth groups, we did it all.

But on the other side of this, despite how hard she tried to protect us from the world, I felt tainted from something that happened to me as a child when she wasn't around. It followed me into my youth and as an adult. It made me feel ugly and

Signs Wonders and Miracles

worthless. I felt like I was nothing my whole life. As a teen, I started to skip school, run away, use drugs and drink. I went to church because she made me.

Then I got pregnant at 15. I turned back to the Lord at that time and tried to be a mom. I worked full time, went to school, etc. But again, I got pulled back into that old life. It got so bad that I was never around my son. He lived with my mom, and I lived life as an addict, making the wrong decisions. I was constantly doing crime and getting arrested. I had criminal charges that were pages long. It was so bad. I was in a bad place in life. I eventually got sober and went back home.

I was 18 when I had my first God encounter. I was being prayed for by my mom's friend. I heard so many voices in my ears, crying, laughing, and sobbing. When he finished praying, I told them what I heard. They heard it too, and that it was my calling.

We found out my mom had stage 4 cancer when I was pregnant with my daughter. I prayed every day for my mom. I prayed for protection for His mercy and grace. Every single day, I prayed for her to get better. When she was on her death bed, I was so mad at God. I didn't understand how He could let her be sick like this. Someone so good, and so pure. I asked Him to give it to me instead, but despite all my tears and prayers, He didn't. I had my daughter Harmony, and when she was 2 months old, we got called to the hospital to say our goodbye's. When we came home that night, I wept and asked God to take me instead, because she deserved life more than me. That night, I had a dream that my daughter died. I knew something was wrong. I tried so hard to wake up, but I couldn't. By the time I did, it was too late. She was gone. My perfect princess was taken from this world. I went numb, I was angry, so angry. I remember praying for God to just give her back and take me. I didn't understand why He was punishing me. That's when I drifted away from God. My mom miraculously got better. The cancer was almost gone, and she seemed good, so I decided to deal with my criminal charges and run away from the rest of my problems.

I went to jail and did 2 years. After being in jail for a few months, I found out I was pregnant again. I delivered my baby in jail. She was born at the time of year my other baby passed away. Exactly one year later, they looked like they were twins. I named her Mercy. I lost custody of her because I was in jail. My sister adopted my kids, so I didn't lose them to the system. I'm more like their auntie now, but we have a great relationship.

My mom ended up passing away while I was in jail. After she passed away, I went to church, to get off the unit and out of my cell. I had an encounter with God there, where God was healing my pain of my daughter, the pain of my mother, and all the things that were hurting inside me.

I'll always remember my last conversation with my mom. She asked me to fix my life when I got out and to do good by my children. So, when I got out, I did exactly that. I haven't touched drugs in over 10 years, but I also quit on God. I do my best to be in my other kid's lives.

God also blessed me with 2 additional beautiful children, Isaiah and Heaven, that I've gotten to raise since birth. I was with their father for five years. I got abused mentally and physically. I was seven months pregnant with our daughter and I was trying to leave him because of the abuse. He held a knife to my throat and his throat and told me that if I left him then one of us wasn't leaving alive, because he wasn't living life without me. He lightly cut my throat and then stabbed himself in the heart twice.

I had to become his home care aide after this, as he had open heart surgery because of the wounds he inflicted on himself. When my daughter was born, he attacked me numerous times. I didn't want another broken family. I wanted to make it work, so I stayed, but I lost myself in the process. I'd cry myself to sleep almost every night, and I'd prepare myself for the abuse that was coming the next day.

My breaking point was when I tried to kill myself over him. I didn't think anyone could ever love me. I thought if I couldn't make him happy, then I'd never make anyone happy.

I woke up one day and realized for our kids' sakes that I needed to leave before he killed one of us. I felt so empty inside. Like something was missing. It didn't matter what I did in life, I was never happy. And here's how I got to where I am now in my journey.

I met this addict randomly. I saw myself in her. She was alone and had no one to lean on. I told her I'd take her in and help her get sober, but that she needed to quit on her own terms. Not even a week later, she took me up on my offer. She quit cold turkey. She moved into my place, and we became friends. She asked me over and over again to go to

The Summit Edmonton Church. I didn't want to go. Then I thought maybe my kids should go, as they are seven and four, and have never been to church before. They went and loved it. So I said I would go the next week, that it couldn't hurt. On November 28, 2021, I went. My friend introduced me to Regina, who asked if she could pray for me. I was unsure but said yes. Regina grabbed my hand and started praying for things she shouldn't know about me. She told me that God wanted my heart. I kept asking how she knew all these things, and she said that she didn't, but that God gave her the words to pray.

I decided I would go again, to see what it all meant. On December 5th, she prayed for me again. This time when I left, I realized I was different. I wanted to keep going to church, for myself. I kept asking what does God expect from me? What does this all mean? How do I even be a Christian? I knew He was real, but that was where it stopped.

I went to a prayer night in the Month of Captivation, the night they were praying for joy. But I felt no joy. The church was full of people dancing, singing, praying, and crying. I saw everyone was into the movement, but I wasn't. I cried and prayed. I wanted to feel what they were feeling. I wanted the joy that everyone was singing about. I felt my wall go up. I felt myself hold back. I was embarrassed and ashamed. I felt like I didn't belong. It took everything inside me to stay and not leave. I felt unworthy, like I was dirt, and no one could see me.

A few days later, I fasted all day and listed to Christian music. When I arrived at prayer for Month of Captivation, my wall was instantly up again. I felt weird and like I didn't belong.

I felt like I needed to speak to the person who was on the microphone praying. Regina and I walked over to her. When I got up to her, she said God wanted my heart. Instantly I started crying. I didn't know why I was crying, but man, I was crying. Tears were pouring out of me, and I was shaking. My legs were weak, my arms were trembling, then I felt all the pain from my childhood pour out of me. All the pain from being abused mentally, sexually, and physically was coming out in my tears. I felt all the guilt, shame, disgust, all the hate for myself, all of it, wash away. I felt my wall drop away, and I felt so many hands on me. So many people were praying for me. When I looked up, I felt loved. I've never felt love before, not because no one loved me, but because I have never let love in. I felt like I didn't deserve to be loved. I felt like I was so ugly and worthless that it wasn't possible to feel loved by anyone. Especially not God.

But in that moment, I felt so loved. For the first time ever, I felt the love from God, from my kids, from my family, from my friends. My heart felt, and still feels full, but it's more than that. For the first time ever in my life, I love God. I love Him so much! I feel beautiful, and free. I don't feel scared of what other people think anymore. I don't feel ashamed to be at church. I don't feel empty anymore. I finally realize what I'm supposed to do and it's this right now. It's to dedicate myself to God and let Him work in me. I'm done being strong. I'm done hiding from fear.

Tonight, I let go of everything and I let Him in, and I'm leaning on Him, I'm trusting in Him. I don't know what my future holds, but He told me it's something big. I feel it in my soul. I know He has something planned for me, and I'm here for all of it. I'm here to listen, pray, worship, and follow this path, wherever it may lead me.

Alice Penner, January 2022

In December of 2020, my family and I found ourselves in a bit of a crisis. My husband had been temporarily laid off in mid November from his construction job, my mom had fallen and broken her foot and was in a cast and on crutches. Then my dad came down with pneumonia which two weeks later was also called Covid.

We had heavy hearts as we began to pray and ask others to pray over our family. We received several incredible answers during that time.

The first was that we felt led to go into business full time as the Lord was leading clients our way. We had already owned a company for exactly 7 years as a side income for when my husband was laid off. I took a step of faith to pursue it full-time to see what the Lord might have in store.

A neighbour who had heard the news of the lay-off called and said, "Open your garage door, I have something to drop off." We went out to the garage afterwards and found a huge table filled with a massive turkey and all the fixings for Christmas breakfast, lunch, supper, dessert, and snacks!

We were in quarantine and the food was so needed but also so unexpected and such a massive gift at that difficult time. God was saying, "I am with you. You can trust me." Even though my neighbour does not know Jesus as her personal saviour, I believe God prompted her to bless us in that way. She said she just felt this incredible urge to do it.

As I mentioned, my dad was quite sick. He ended up at the University Hospital in the ICU on a ventilator. I asked my friend Colleen if she would please pray. Many others who also know my parents were praying. Colleen happened to be headed into a Firewall prayer call at that time. It was around lunch time and in that call, Colleen was prompted to pray not just for my dad but for my entire family. The prayer team that hour agreed with the prayer and prayed strengthening for us as well.

If you ask Colleen how it went, she will tell you that she felt a sticky-honey feeling come over her hands as the Lord alighted on her as she prayed. The prayer was answered directly that day. My dad made a huge turn around starting that afternoon and was out of ICU by Monday.

However, I would fail to give God full glory if I didn't mention that we had four other miracles happen in our family at the same time that same day!

Miracle 2: My Mom's broken foot stopped being swollen and she noticed later that day that she was not experiencing any pain at all as she had her air cast off. She started testing it out and soon realized that God had shortened her 8-week healing in a cast down to just 2 weeks. She didn't need the cast after that.

Miracle 3: My daughter had been suffering for quite some time with some pretty intense back and neck pain. Her back and neck pain went completely away that day and has never returned.

Miracle 4: My daughter also had an extra tooth in her mouth that we were discussing having pulled. It miraculously fell out that afternoon! We put it in a bag and hung it on the fridge and called it the miracle tooth. God cares about the little things that matter to us, even a little unwanted tooth.

Miracle 5: Lastly, I had been experiencing some pains in my chest that week as I would breathe in and out on the top right side of my lungs. Those pains disappeared all at once that afternoon. Just gone, never to return.

Christmas was pretty special to us in 2020 as we celebrated literally all that God had done to touch our lives.

The neat part was that God was just getting started in showing His glory in our lives as we began 2021. We continued to experience blessings, breakthroughs and three more healings.

Here are a few more stories from 2021 in our family where we were touched by heaven.

We had not been attending in-person at Summit Church but had only begun our connection there online. Each Sunday morning our little family of 5 would gather down in our basement which we'd be sure to make clean and ready for 'church' each week. One morning I felt the urge to bring oil down and anoint the space to set it apart as a house of praise.

During another Sunday morning service in the basement, the Holy Spirit touched me, and I felt such a heaviness come over me that was so strong my legs went limp, and I fell down to the ground; my mind was with the Holy Spirit. My family had no idea what had just happened and neither did I. That had never happened to me before, and I didn't even know what it was. I called my friend Colleen later that day and she explained to me that it was Holy Spirit doing some work in my life.

The basement had a different feeling after that, and we all started to be more tuned in to what was happening in our lives spiritually.

The next time that happened to me in the basement, my mouth was filled with foreign words. It was all very bizarre to me as we had not experienced that at any other churches. Holy Spirit was personally bringing me along in things. My little family was on their knees that day as we submitted to Holy Spirit for the first time as a whole group. God was doing things in my husband and my daughter's heart as well that day.

In June 2021, my daughter Chloe had this incredible urge to go to the East location to attend Youth group. She knew no one. We had never been to The Summit Edmonton Church in person, we had only watched online. My daughter is pretty shy, but in this case a boldness came over her and she insisted we drive her in to the East end from our hometown of Devon.

We arrived, and she went in. God was beckoning us all in, through her. That next Sunday we finally attended for the first time over at the West location after more than 9 months watching online. It was good to go in person and begin to connect with our new "family".

I had an experience at the West location when we were meeting in the Courtyard by Marriot. One day in July, my husband Mike and I had gone forward for prayer at the end of the service. A young man named Dillon prayed over our business. We went back to our seats, and I felt a heaviness come over my legs and a pressure that was so intense, I could not stand up any longer. I started sinking to the floor, but I kept resisting it because shame was speaking to me. The service ended and people were starting to visit. What was happening to me was not in sync with what was happening in the room. I persisted in trying to pull myself back up to my feet, but something kept pushing me back down. It was bizarre, so I finally stopped wrestling with God and got down and just listened.

God had new things for me after that. My husband eventually had to help me walk to the car as my legs were so weak that I could hardly stand or walk. It was surreal to say the least. My walk with God deepened and soon I started experiencing dreams and visions from God like never before. Oh Lord you are so good. I give You all the glory!

My older sister, Cara, came from Calgary a couple of times as a visitor to Summit West. On Thanksgiving Sunday, she was visiting and there was a special miracle that took place. The previous spring, Cara had had an injury to her knee and a hard, thick band had formed across the top of her knee. She had X-rays and treatments, but nobody seemed to know where this hard band of tissue had come from or how to get rid of it. They did know it was not cancerous, but it was impeding movement. She described it like the band was acting like a brace and keeping her knee immobile. She was also experiencing a form of inversion when she would walk up stairs or hills. Her knee would start to go backward as a result of all the pressure from the front and this terrible band.

On Thanksgiving, Cara went forward for prayer at the altar. The prayer ministry person wrapped her loving arms around my sister and prayed over her. Cara went home and later that day noticed that something was different with her knee. The band was not hard, but rather squishy and a bit soft for the first time.

She drove home to Calgary, and the next day the band was softer and squishier. Then by Wednesday it had all but disappeared from above her knee.

Cautiously testing it out she realized that her knee was no longer inverting when she'd go up and down the stairs and the pain she'd experienced from doing stairs was no longer there. She is still a bit cautious with her knee but can not help but give God glory that the entire hard band is gone and has never returned and that doing stairs is not a fearful thing anymore.

We have had other moments where God alighted and did things in 2021 over our family. It was truly a year of touches from heaven, and we are all changed for having been given the opportunity to experience them. Thank you Lord.

Tracy Weselowski, January 2021

Testimonies About Healing

I've had allergies my entire life. I've prayed for healing more times than I can count. Over the years, I have received a measure of healing, but still the allergies remain. On Sunday, November 8, 2020, I got ready for church, and on the ride to church, I started feeling strange. By the time I arrived, as the church service was starting, I knew I was having an allergic reaction. I could tell it was bad and realized that it was about to get anaphylactic. My husband began telling me it was time to go to the hospital. He asked me to pull out my epi-pen. I hesitated because I hate doing both of those things. After an epi-pen, I always feel like I've been run over by a truck. Instead, I texted my co-workers (pastoral staff) and told them what was happening. Three of them came running to pray for me. They prayed and declared that the allergic reaction would stop.

As they prayed, they also asked me questions, and helped reveal a lie I believed. The lie I believed was that I was only valuable when there was a problem. This took me back to my childhood where I felt I only got attention when something was wrong, like when I was having an allergic reaction. I then acknowledged the truth, which is that I matter all the time. Very quickly, the allergic reaction began to subside. I felt the swelling decreasing in my throat, in my eyes, in my face. The reaction stopped. My inner healing manifested in my outer healing. In all the years that I had asked God for healing, I had believed that I wasn't healed because I wasn't valuable and didn't matter, when really the truth was that the allergies were what Jesus was trying to use to expose the lie in my life.

Once the lie was revealed, the anaphylaxis stopped. I am no longer afraid of allergies or anaphylaxis, because I know that when I see God and myself rightly, there is nothing to fear.

Tracy Belford, November 2020

In March 2020, I was scheduled to go for an inner healing and freedom session. Two days before that everything got shut down due to COVID and my session was postponed. Jesus had been preparing my heart for inner healing, and when my session was postponed, I decided maybe I should get some professional help as well. I had a referral from a friend for a Holy Spirit filled counselor and I decided to make an appointment. Jesus obviously had a plan for my healing because my counselor and I partnered with Him to do some inner healing. It was incredible what happened in just a few months. When I first started counseling, I was in a frozen state, not able to feel or express my emotions well. I was so locked up. Beginning with sexual abuse by my neighbour at the age of 7, there were other traumas that compounded the pain and caused anxiety and depression. My heart was buried under so many layers. But Jesus took my frozen, traumatized heart and began to soften it. I actually had a picture of me giving Jesus my heart. He held it in His hands and was rubbing oil into it; when it was soft and all the cracks were filled in, He handed it back to me.

In July 2020, I was in the middle of my healing journey, and I had a fall off a ladder and injured my spine and ended up with a concussion. I had persistent concussive symptoms including light sensitivity, headaches, sensitivity to loud noises and neck pain that continued for about 7 months. I had seen a concussion specialist, gone to the chiropractor as well as physio and things were slowly improving but it was still really affecting my quality of life.

In January 2021, I was at my aunt's house, and I told her I had a headache that day. She asked if she could pray for me. She told me she had been reading about a spirit of trauma and she asked if it would be alright if she prayed over me. I agreed, and as soon as she touched me and prayed, my headache instantly went away and so did the tension in my neck. I felt the trauma leave along with my concussion symptoms. At the chiropractor the next day, he noticed that I had a huge improvement in my neck mobility and back and asked me what changed, and I gave Jesus all the credit! I also went to my physiotherapy appointment where I was retested and passed all the vestibular focus testing with better results than most people without any injuries.

In February 2021, I had my inner healing and freedom session at The Summit Edmonton Church. Jesus healed me from a few different things. My maternal grandfather was involved with Freemasonry, and I wanted to get freedom from those curses. Among the many curses I was set free from was a curse on the thyroid. I had Hashimoto's Thyroiditis, an auto immune disease that attacks your thyroid. Another curse that affected me was the spirit of death, which caused Sleep Apnea. I had also had a gall bladder attack in December and that was also one of the curses. Praise Jesus I am free from that now as well! Jesus set me free of the curses of Freemasonry and I no longer have Hashimoto's Thyroiditis or Sleep Apnea or gallbladder pain. I am no longer living my life exhausted and traumatized anymore.

Thank you, Jesus. I am continually being undone by your goodness and love towards me.

Jacqueline Lefebvre, February 2021

Throughout 2020 God started speaking to me about my hearing. In 2013, I was diagnosed by an ENT as having major hearing loss due to the trauma incurred through years of domestic abuse, but the 3 bones inside my ear were completely broken and calcified together, rendering them useless. Not even a hearing aid would give me hearing I was told. I could not hear low tones (men with deep voices or if my back was to someone). If there was any background noise, I had to resort to reading lips and strain to hear, turning my head to the right so my left ear could pick up the words people were speaking. I was waiting for 10% more hearing loss and to become a certain age, so that doctors could even think about taking bones from a cadaver and placing them into my ear.

By January 2021, I was alone with the Lord when He started to tell me how He had a new set of ears for me if I would just believe Him. He showed me a room in heaven where many new body parts were, including my new ears. He started showing me how to 'work' the word in faith. I chose to stand in faith at that moment and receive the new ear God told me He had for me.

I attended the Summit, by invite, for the first time on April 27th, 2021. It was announced that God wanted to heal ears that had been damaged and immediately without hesitation, I looked at the person who invited me and I quietly yelled in his face "That's me!" I knew that I knew, that I knew I had to take by faith in that moment the promise that God had spoken to me. Someone came over and prayed for me and all I did was just receive. I heard some crackling going on in my ear for a bit as the service started. During the service I was listening to the pastor preach and all of a sudden it dawned on me. I leaned over to the friend who had invited me, and I said "Um, is there always a keyboard playing when your pastor is preaching?" He actually didn't know as he said he never noticed before. Well, I noticed because I wasn't reading the pastors lips, and music was playing in the background. The pastor's low tone superseded the sound of the high pitch keyboard, and I heard him clear as day. This blew me away because previously I could not hear low tones and if there was background noise, I might as well re-watch a service because I would have missed many parts of the preaching. I inquired of the Lord on this, and He said, "Kelly, I wanted to show you that you are healed, and this was a perfect way."

Kelly Lamanteer, April 2021

One Sunday on night shift, I cut all the layers of the skin on my finger, and it was as wide as a fingernail. I just missed my muscle, you could see the muscle and the insides of my finger, it was pretty nasty.

I prayed as I was in the medical room. There wasn't a lot of blood coming out, just a little bit, which was impressive. I didn't go to the doctor, instead I went to see my mom. She said I didn't need stitches, and I didn't want stitches, so I just let it heal and prayed that I wouldn't lose my finger to an infection.

A week later, it was just about sealed up. People kept asking me, "Was it deep, did you get stitches?" I said that I did not get stitches. I just knew the skin cells would seal and glue themselves back together, and they did. God's creation is so good. Even though there was medical intervention later, God was still able to move in my initial healing process.

Kaisha Whatman, August 2021

I have always felt the Holy Spirit at The Summit Edmonton Church, but I haven't been there for a while because of a jaw infection. I attended the West location one Sunday. I felt so heavy from the Holy Spirit's presence that I could barely stand. God's presence was there. I was in awe of the prayer team, and it brought tears to my eyes to see all the elementary school kids up there worshipping God!

I went up for breakthrough prayer and when the prayer team laid hands on me, I didn't just shake like I do when someone anointed lays hands on me. I am sure I saw and felt God's glory! I could barely stand. My body got so hot and it felt like electric currents were running through me from head to toe! As more hands were laid on me, there was a light around me, and I ended up falling backwards to the ground. Thank you to the team members that caught me. I know my breakthrough that I have been praying for 15 years is starting, praise God. I received healing of my carpal tunnel syndrome that day. I haven't worn my braces since. I couldn't write or sleep without them. Now I have no need of them.

I have been crying out to God for a long time, but it has intensified in the last two weeks. I have become desperate, so I started reading chapters of my Bible daily and immersing myself in Godly things like listening to praise and worship. I've always felt the Holy Spirit during worship at the Summit, but something has changed. I have never felt God's presence or the Holy Spirit's like this last Sunday. The best way to explain it is that the air was thick and heavy. I believe we are experiencing the revival we have been praying for. I'm so glad I finally was able to go to church that day after two months in bed!

Michelle Koziak Maynard, November 2021

We got to pray for a stranger, Russ, at Home Depot. It was really incredible! He had something wrong with his leg and so Vivian and I approached him and started talking to him, briefly to kind of explain things, and then we started praying.

He started saying, "Oh, whoa whoa! What is that?" He had a physical manifestation of an experience with God in the middle of Home Depot.

Mike Miketon, November 2021

I was going to buy a car. And the sales guy said, "Oh, my back hurts." I said, "Well, before we get started with this car deal, let me pray for you." I prayed, and the car salesman got healed. Previously, he had to sit crouched over the sink for 30 minutes each day, just to get through the day because of the back pain. When God healed him, he said, "I don't know what happened but it's amazing!"

Josh Mellot, November 2021

On a Sunday, a person at church released a word about a sickness in someone's body regarding flow of blood to the heart. I sensed it was for me, but I didn't have that issue. I thought it was for a friend because this friend had heart issues after she had COVID. I wanted to go up and receive the word. The person who released the word said that the person with the issue did not know about the illness.

A few weeks later I found out that I have low iron which was quite severe symptomatically. I then knew the word was for me. The next Sunday I told the woman who released the word. Some people prayed over me, and my symptoms left me at that moment. I just started feeling better and better- headache, brain fog, joint pain, extreme fatigue left my body.

Laurika Booysen, November 2021

God did a miracle! I have been praying for a little girl in Pakistan. I am friends with a Pastor of an underground church in Pakistan. He reached out for prayer because his youngest daughter, Nayab, had an accident at home with a knife. It went directly into her eye. The family rushed her to the public hospital where they received some care, but the eye was blind. They were praying for a miracle. They know there was a surgery available they could undergo, but it could only be done at the private US based hospital in Pakistan.

Then God did a miracle for that little girl. Her father said, "God has answered your prayer and my daughter Nayab has started seeing blocks of light. When I checked with the doctor today, she said that God has done a miracle!"

Tracy Weselowski, December 2021

I was on a ventilator for 34 days and in hospital for 55 days. I was diagnosed with COVID on September

7, 2021 and stayed at home for the week. However, I wasn't getting any better. My oxygen levels were very low at 67 and I thought there was something wrong with my oxygen reader.

I was lying in the bedroom chair when out of the blue Kelsey, my daughter, said to me that Elaine called and said I needed to go to the hospital. Elaine is a client of Cerulean Boutique, a doctor, and has had long haul COVID. She is a woman of great faith and said she heard from God to phone me to go to the hospital.

Kelsey, my daughter, also had COVID, and was lying in bed so she phoned Braden, my son, to come and take me to the hospital. When I arrived, I was told I had to be intubated. I was alone due to COVID protocols, so I phoned Kelsey and Braden and told them that I was being intubated, then passed out from lack of oxygen. I was later told that if I had left it moments longer, I would have had brain damage as I was at 44 % oxygen level.

I was in a coma and could hear the people around me laughing and talking. The doctors had me on fentanyl and oxycontin to sedate me. I had high anxiety, and the doctors did not know how to handle it, so they continued to give me hallucinating drugs. As long as I was on the drugs, I was not able to breathe for myself. During this time, the doctor told Kelsey and Braden that I was dying, that I had a secondary infection, and that I wouldn't make it. I had many people praying for my recovery, more than I could have imagined. To this day I find friends that say they were praying for recovery.

I was dying on my way to heaven when I asked the Holy Spirit if I really had to go. He said, "You are pretty far gone." "Why now?" I said. "I know but I just found you." I told Him that I wanted to be a grandma for my grandchildren. Their other grandmother died this year. It wasn't good that they would not have a grandmother to guide and teach them. I told Holy Spirit I wanted to live into my 90's, sit with friends and family. I had a lot to live for. He told me that there would be things to overcome. I agreed and said that I would be a testimony of His healing.

Kelsey was my power of attorney and she said to take me off the drugs. The nurses did not like to be told what to do so they went cold turkey, and I was breathing at 70 breaths per minute. They were manipulating and punitive. Kelsey stayed by my side until my heart and breath stabilized. They were giving me dairy and wheat which my system could not tolerate well, and I was having trouble getting well. Kelsey noticed this and then they gave me vegetable mix. I regained consciousness on October 11, 2021. I have no idea about when I spoke with the Holy Spirit and when I came out of the coma.

I had many wonderful Holy Spirit visits while in the hospital. I couldn't talk for 34 days. My hands were tied to the bed. I prayed and reflected on my life. When I got off the ventilation, my right lung collapsed, and they had to do a reverse suction to inflate the lung. It was supposed to be a 5-day fix. The doctors had to put a tube in for reverse suction. Kelsey and Braden were the only ones allowed in the room. They came and laid hands on my lungs and began to pray. The hole in my lung healed overnight and I was starting my recovery.

The pain was very intense. The medication was not relieving the pain so I would hold on to Jesus' coat and ask for the pain to go. Immediately the pain would lift, and I was able to rest. I asked for relief many times and each time He helped me.

It was during this time that I asked God for complete healing, and the Holy Spirit said to get up and dance. I know I could have but the nurses were worried that I would get up in the night and my tube would come out, so they fenced me in the bed.

The hospitals keep people alive with medication and science. There is no room for faith in the hospital. After knowing that I would be completely healed, I would not let the doctors speak negatively over me. Several doctors came daily to give me my diagnosis. I told them not to tell me anymore. I only wanted to know if it was the same or better. One respiratory therapist told me that I could recover, and that I needed to get cardio.

I was discharged on November 7, 2021. I have been home for 3 months now and am still recovering.

I am off assisted oxygen and able to move around the house. Every day and every week are marked improvements and by spring I will be outside walking and riding my bicycle.

Jill Bulmer, January 2022

In early October my wife Karen and I tested positive for COVID, and I became weaker as the days went by. On October 13th, a Christian friend who I had pastored as a teenager years ago, now worked at Grey Nuns Hospital, and learning of my weakened condition felt to come and check on me. He stopped by our Prayer Clinic as I was preparing for a Zoom Meeting, took my vitals, and called 911 to have me immediately transported to Emergency. He later told me in his years of experience in ICU, he believed there was a 1 in 50 chance that I would make it. I later read in a publication by Mayo Clinic that for people younger, and with stronger stats then I, had a .08% of survival.

My blood oxygen level had dropped to 42%. Rachel, my daughter, arrived from Egypt and posted on Facebook a call for earnest fervent intercession for God to spare my life. The Summit Edmonton Church immediately mobilized such prayer along with many others.

The medical team placed me on 'Comfort Care'. Karen called our family as they did not expect me to make it through the night.

On October 20th the doctors realized I was being sustained by non-medical intervention. I was able to receive the maximum possible oxygen feed. I began to slowly recover but had one more serious relapse.

With continued updates posted on Facebook the intercessors travailed and prevailed. Hundreds of people were praying for me. I was eventually transferred to recovery, and my oxygen supplements were gradually reduced to a minimum.

On November 25th, I had a parade of doctors, nurses and medical staff come by my room to congratulate me on being released. A number of them, even as non-believers in Christ, commented it was only because of prayer to God that I was alive.

I know I am a living miracle attributed only to the healing mercy of our Lord Jesus Christ, in response to the intercessory prayers that were mingled together with the incense of worship on the golden altar before the Throne of Grace of our Heavenly Father.

Thank you, Summit Church, for each and every faithful intercessor who held my life before our Lord. I also want to personally thank Pastor Nikki and her parents, Jeff and Dianne Hilton, for their years of faithful love and prayer for me as their former pastor.

Revelation 8:3-4 (NLT) *"Then another angel with a gold incense burner came and stood at the altar. And a great amount of incense was given to him to mix with the prayers of God's people as an offering on the gold altar before the throne. The smoke of the incense, mixed with the prayers of God's holy people, ascended up to God from the altar where the angel had poured them out."*

Psalm 141:1-2 (NLT) *"O Lord, I am calling to you. Please hurry! Listen when I cry to you for help! Accept my prayer as incense offered to you, and my upraised hands as an evening offering."*

Bob Gal, November 2021

Testimonies About Houses

We were selling my Father-in-Law's patio-home after he passed away. Our Christian realtor listed the house quite low for the market to try and encourage a frenzy of people to look at it. We were expecting that the house would sell within a week as most houses have been selling in a week or less. I decided to look up scriptures and took the house that correlated to the house number (1232) then pray for the sale according to the scriptures I found.

I then texted the following to our realtor:

"Hi BJ. How is it going? Has there been any interest generated? As we are driving home, I decided to find scriptures that correlated to the address of Dad's home. What I found was these scriptures"

John 12:32 *And I, if I am lifted up from the earth, will draw all people to Myself.*

Deuteronomy 12:32 *Whatever I command you, be careful to observe it; you shall not add to it nor take away from it.*

1 Chron 12:32a *of the sons of Issachar who had understanding of the times, to know what Israel ought to do...*

I prayed, "Father may we magnify You in all we do, lifting up the name of Jesus and giving Him glory for the testimony of your goodness and may it draw people to you. May BJ, Jeff and I have wisdom and understanding to know the 'times'/direction as did the tribe of Issachar for Israel, and may we be ready, willing, and careful to hear Your voice/direction not adding or taking away from it. Amen."

I closed the text by writing, "Thank you, BJ, for being a voice for the Lord in the marketplace."

We expected multiple offers, but by Tuesday we had not one offer, which the realtor was astounded at. Then on Tuesday a bully offer came in for $80,000 more than the asking price, which was a fantastic price for that home. The people who put in the offer had no idea there had been no other offers. Because houses had been selling quickly and above market value, in order to secure the house, the buyers gave a very high offer that had to be accepted by 6pm or the deal was off (bully offer). Since there had been no other offers (which was so unusual) and it was such a great offer, we jumped on it! It was definitely an over and above blessing from the Lord, we thank Him and give God all the glory.

Dianne Hilton, August 2021

My House Testimony- I was initially hesitant as a recently self-employed single woman (in other words, a variable sole income) but with the encouragement of friends, and the leading of the Lord, I began looking around for a house (I was renting an apartment previously). Once I actually started looking, it all happened so quickly, and obstacles came down!

Within a week of searching online I went to a viewing of 4 houses. 'My' house was among these 4. I went with 2 friends to see it. My friends, realtor, and I immediately knew upon seeing this home that this was the one.

At the same time, I was in the midst of looking at financing, talking to a couple banks and a mortgage broker. As stated above, financially I was in a questionable position (recently self-employed and single/sole income). By traditional means, I would not qualify for the level of financing and mortgage I needed. But I kept talking to these mortgage specialists. They came to understand my situation and wanted to help me find a way to make it work. As I continued to talk with them, an exception was found for me and a week after that first viewing, I was pre-approved for the amount of mortgage I needed, and with an excellent interest rate.

That same day I went for a second viewing and immediately placed an offer. The sellers responded quickly, and agreement was reached, set just below the financing I was pre-approved for. Additionally, the sellers volunteered HALF their furniture and ALL their garden tools! These were all high-quality items. (It turns out the sellers were moving to Vancouver and downsizing). This was a blessing beyond anything I imagined! I was moving out of a small apartment with minimal furniture.

In addition, this house had the potential for an additional source of income by renting out the basement. Again, with a variable sole income, this was a big deal - God provided the opportunity for a secondary source.

I moved in a month and a half later. The house has already been a huge blessing to me. Not just in it being already partly furnished etc., but in the midst of hardship in other areas of life, it's been such a safe haven to me; a place to press into the Lord. And I know it'll continue to be a blessing as I intend to use this home towards fellowship. Thank you, God.

Janet K, July 2021

Testimonies About Finances

I moved to Edmonton into an adult building in March 2021. My daughter lives in Calgary with my grandsons and due to unforeseen circumstances, I've had one of my grandsons come to live with me. My landlord had allowed him to visit me before with the understanding that it was an adult building, and my grandson was a visitor. However, this time my grandson will be staying with me for an unforeseen length of time. When I found this out, I panicked. I knew that my building was an adult only building, so I was looking to move. I asked my landlord for time so I could look for a place and money for a damage deposit. I was pleading with Jesus to help me find a new home and money. I prayed for open doors.

My landlord called me a few weeks ago saying that my grandson could stay! My landlord spoke to the other tenants, and they agreed to let my grandson stay. It was with the signed understanding for 2 months. I signed an agreement to this. God is so good and softened the hearts of my landlord AND tenants.

Now, my daughter needs me to care for my grandson longer and I may have to move so I was apartment hunting...again. I just spoke to my landlord through text, and he says that I could possibly stay till my lease runs out which is next March. I'm in awe! I saw this as an impossible situation. I have never heard of a landlord giving a tenant this much grace. Especially in an adult building.

I prayed for open doors and God opened hearts. Thank You Papa.

Iris Gibot, August 2021

To understand our journey, you need to understand a bit about us. We are Lisa and Rick Walmsley, together for just over 20 years.

Lisa's relationship with God is lifelong and includes a recently renewed and far more emotional calling to faith than Rick's. Rick's faith story is one of waning and waxing and far more academic in approach. Between the two of them, they compliment each other's views and round out a healthy appreciation of our Lord.

Some years ago, Lisa developed a medical condition that although not life threatening, does prevent her from working. Rick's employment was stable with a good income and benefits until that changed abruptly and unexpectedly in 2017. Rick had invested years in educating himself and working countless overtime hours in hopes of being able to make a difference when the opportunity came. The opportunity was delivered in 2015, but changes in corporate ownership structure and attitudes eliminated his position with little regard for any length of service or efforts given towards the company.

All was not dire as the severance package was a year's salary paid out over time requiring little change to lifestyle and a decent enough length of time to find a new position; or so we thought. Lisa's condition also qualifies her to collect a modest pension and our adult son who lives at home contributes rent which does help out. The first few months of unemployment were a bit of a mourning period with the usual anger, grief and frustration while feeling discarded and undervalued. Once that resolved itself, we enjoyed the Christmas season of 2017 with friends and family with still no real worries for the future. With the holiday season over, the work of seeking out new employment began in earnest.

What we soon found out was that the market had changed significantly in oil and gas and the global downturn in commodity pricing had caused extensive layoffs and restructuring throughout the industry. The next several months were a vast series of applications and networking efforts that yielded few if any replies or even acknowledgements of applications. Several positions applied for that never responded were reposted without any notification regarding the first application and the same for any subsequent application.

By August of 2018, the severance package was set to expire, and employment prospects were not looking good. Rick had EI to fall back on and had gone to the Service Canada center to inquire about the process and severance package details when he was first laid off in 2017. What we didn't know at that time was that the process he was told to follow was completely wrong and when he applied after the severance money stopped coming in, he was categorically denied.

Undaunted, the appeals process began which we also found out was the incorrect approach to take in this circumstance after going through it twice. Several months later with our savings dwindling, Rick received a phone call from a federal employee based out of Vancouver who had his file come across her desk. This woman was a blessing. She listened to the whole story from the beginning, took a few notes and assured us that this was far from an isolated instance.

A month or so passed until she called back explaining that there had been a lot of EI misinformation regarding the treatment of claims with severance packages. She asked for our patience while she processed the requisite paperwork to correct the original oversight. A few weeks later she called to inform us that all was good, and we would be receiving EI. She actually completed the entire series of by-weekly card questions with Rick over the phone. So much time had passed that the first EI payment was for nearly 75% of the entire claim eligibility.

This might seem an inconsequential series of events to most but by the end of this testimony you will realize it was undoubtedly our Lord proving himself by providing for us at what seemed like nearly the last moment.

EI provided another cushion to carry on in our search for employment. Our lifestyle had to undergo some changes to live on a very tight budget. By this point we had sent out a few hundred applications with less than a 1% response of any kind. It was becoming very depressing because of the education, experience, and qualifications Rick had. We started applying for just about anything with a reasonable income level that was in any way relatable to his qualifications.

Our lifestyle now incorporated a monthly application to the Food Bank and most any gifting for our grandchildren was through the vast array of thrift shops in the Edmonton area. It is our fortunate experience to note the charity of strangers in donating so many new or like new items to the various thrift shops. Our children, grandchildren and other close family and friends graciously received these gifts with no knowledge of their origins. Beans, pasta, and soups were far more routine dinners than ever before. We felt then a sense of humility that none of what we gave up living so modestly was really that hard to part with in the first place.

Lisa's involvement at The Summit Edmonton Church had grown including a strong calling to participate in missions work, something she had desired to do since her teens. We saw no need to postpone or otherwise not heed this calling. We began letting go of many material items we had acquired through the years, and thanks to the online marketplace, Lisa essentially ran a cottage enterprise selling off our excess to provide the majority of the funding for her missions' trips. A huge shout out to the Summit family and other family and friends who also gave in support of her missions' trips as we simply couldn't have done this without you. It was amazing to find how much stuff we had gathered through the years that was so easy to let go of thanks to a little push in the direction of faith.

Lisa made it her personal mission to collect backpacks for the children of the Sao Paulo favellas. Her inability to speak the language did not stop her from hugging, loving, and praying over everyone she met on these missions. Lisa has now been to Sao Paulo twice and New Orleans once with the Missions Team. She has returned each time filled with a renewed spirit that was worth all the penny pinching required to get her there and is regularly in contact with people in Sao Paulo weekly.

In November of 2018, Lisa heard a word that God was handpicking a new position for Rick, that it may not happen that year and to be patient. Just before Christmas of 2018, Rick was contacted by a recruiting agency for a position in Ft. McMurray with an extensive interview process complete with 3rd party psychometric testing which began on January 4th of 2019. After flying through the testing, multiple interviews and Rick's references being contacted, we were brought up to Ft. McMurray in April at the company's expense so Rick could meet the team, tour the facilities, and spend an entire day in interviews with the various people he would be working with. Surely, we thought this must be the job Lisa had heard about.

Through this process we had planned and budgeted for Rick to rent a place in Ft. McMurray and come home on weekends and any other opportunities, as the job was a Monday to Friday work week. We knew it would be tough but were in no way prepared to sell our home in Edmonton or take Lisa away from our grandchildren.

Not long after returning to Edmonton we received word that the company had decided to go in another direction. We were in shock. Lisa heard a whisper from God "Lisa, my intention is not to have you living separately."

Since the initial layoff, Rick had maintained his volunteer committee work for the sake of the network connections and had received a few leads and even an interview through this network. It was now the middle of 2019 and the EI money had also dried up. One of the network connections with the Government of Alberta approached Rick's committee to perform some research under a grant program. Rick and one other committee member completed the application process and once again at the eleventh hour, the grant funding was approved.

Rick re-established his own long dormant registered business looking to offer some consulting services which was required in order to manage the flow of grant monies for the work performed. This was a small price to pay to ensure another source of income. Little did we know at the time how much of a blessing this set of circumstances was going to be.

The grant money provided a stable though budget conscious income, throughout the fall of 2019 and the spring of 2020. Twice, the Lord (for who else could have seen the approaching ruin and prevented it) provided for us.

With the grant funded project wrapping up and the monies collected and expended, early 2020 was beginning to look promising. Additional grant monies were being discussed and applied for with expansions on the original work and opportunities elsewhere.

In early 2020, we had been hearing about a new pneumonia like disease originating out of Wuhan, China but didn't have any concept of how this was about to impact everyone's lives. It was with surreal disbelief that we watched the news change from a viral threat to a global pandemic. The closing of borders, stay at home orders and a general state of confusion over the nature of this virus was an ocean of misinformation that has not settled out to this day. Any talk of grant funded projects, consulting opportunities or conventional employment quickly evaporated as the Corona virus we know as Covid-19 began to take hold of the world. Our situation went from one of trepidatious optimism to near-dire collapse once again.

Remember how Rick had to ramp up his own business to work with the provincial grant money? The net result when Covid support programs emerged was that his once active business stopped dead due to Covid. We qualified for the CERB and later CRB as the business fit the criteria and had generated enough income from sources proven to have dried up due to the pandemic.

This is now three times our Lord has pulled us from the brink and intervened to keep us whole, and at this point we have completely given in to his influence. And yet there is still more to come. Throughout 2020, we stayed at home, followed the guidelines, sanitized, washed our hands, and pretty much kept to ourselves. The economics of our existence over the past few years had already limited our outings and interactions, but we were humbled to a degree we had never known before.

In January of 2021, Lisa asked Rick if he had actually prayed or asked God for favour in helping find work. Rick had only dealt with this in very general terms. Rick was reminded to take the time to have a conversation with our Lord, a bit of "Ask and you shall receive" as it were.

As 2020 turned to 2021, Covid relief funding remained our only real source of income beyond Lisa's pension and our son's rent. When the spring crunch of home and car insurance, winter heating bills, etc. hit, we were able to meet these expenses, but our well was truly dry. Lisa humbly confided in the Summit Church, and they came through for us in our time of need, helping out with grace and charity. Again, we were humbled and owe all the Summit family a huge shout out again. With summer coming and Covid support payments about to expire, the government announced an extended program that would reduce benefits but continue until the end of September.

This would now be the fourth time our future looked so completely uncertain and grim and yet we were saved again. Praise be to God!

At the near end of our rope and still trying to remain positive and upbeat while filling out online profiles and continually editing and updating resumes and cover letters, on June 21st, Rick came across an ad for a new position with a company he had a networking connection with. He spent over an hour creating an online profile (a fairly common occurrence these days), attached his resume and a cover letter and clicked on "Submit" with no expectations that this time would be any different. He then reached out by email to his network contact just to advise that he had applied and would be appreciative of any recommendation or assistance his contact could provide.

Within 3 hours of his application and before his network contact even replied to his email, the phone rang with a request for a screening interview that week. The screening interview led to a more formal team interview. The team interview led to a second. The second was followed by an offer of employment that same day. So anxious was this company to hire Rick and trusting of his qualification and network contact impression that they didn't even ask for references. August 3rd, 2021, Rick went back to work after 4 years. We have full benefits in place from day one, and our income is right back to the level commensurate with his experience and qualifications.

The only reason Rick's start date was Tuesday, August 3rd was simply that the preceding Monday, August 2nd was a holiday. This is worth mention and observation as it was Lisa who first noticed that the severance payments from Rick's initial layoff had actually ceased on August 2nd of 2018. Our first assisted steps out of the desert had been given to us exactly three years to the day that our struggles had truly begun.

This last miracle (and we cannot deny the miraculous nature of these events) was the fifth time we approached the brink and looked into the chasm, only to be saved each time. It gets better. The night that the offer was made just happened to be a Friday that the Summit was having an evening worship event. We couldn't wait to attend, share our good news and give out a few huge hugs to those who had supported us in faith and otherwise.

During our lean years, Lisa had also lost a dental crown in 2017 and had begun to experience some uncomfortable dental pain. With benefits being an immediate perk of new employment, she booked the first available appointment and we braced for some bad news. Other than a bit of cleaning, only the crown repair is required and all else is fine.

We continue to find blessings after leaving the desert but vow to remain humbled by the experience and more giving and thoughtful towards others in need. Though our journey through the desert is over we are ever mindful of those still lost and struggling and will do what we can to offer direction and support. Lisa is also looking forward to being able to participate in any upcoming missions.

Blessing to all who've been on this journey with us, supported us spiritually or otherwise and kept faith throughout.

Lisa and Rick Walmsley, August 2021

We have an awesome financial testimony! Days before the year's end we received a message from our bookkeeper that we were $3600 in the hole for a project. My heart sank as I read the message because I wasn't sure how this could turn around in such a short time. "Lord, we don't know what you're going to do here" were the simple words uttered from our lips as we tried to muster up our prayer in faith. We knew God was able, and yet felt the wind dissipating from our sails. A few days went by, and we received another message that said, "We are getting closer." A little money had trickled in. We prayed again and although we were still a few thousand away from our goal, We said, "Lord, this is in your hands. We're not striving in this; you've got to do this because we surely can't." A few hours later, we received another message saying another $200 had come in. We thanked the Lord. We were celebrating over every bit that was coming in! Another message came through, "Another $500" and then, "Another $3400" and then, "Another 100" and hours before the final deadline another $1000 had come in. We went from going into the new year with a deficit, to going into the new year with money in the bank to dream for what was to come! It was one of those times we had to choose to surrender and trust Him from a position of rest, not striving, knowing if it was His vision He would surely provide.

Heather Paton, December 2021

Testimonies From the Wise Money Course

We didn't realize that by attending the Wise Money financial course, we would also get a church family that we've grown to love and appreciate so much.

Using the principles taught in this course, we were able to pay off over $15K in debt, and actually have a savings account now. We would highly recommend this course to anyone interested in their finances. Whether you're in debt, newly married, or have had a significant event in your life that affects your financial situation, this course is incredibly encouraging and life-giving.

Caley and Blake Sovdi, April 2021

During the Wise Money class, I received multiple things- friends, wisdom, and clarity. I was 20K in debt that really stemmed from laziness in not taking care of my expenses and having little value on money management. Within a couple of months of starting the class, I had cleared that up and gotten debt free. More than that though, I received the framework for making decisions about how to spend money founded on the biblical principle that a debtor is a slave. A SLAVE. I came to know Christ and being a slave was not on my list of things I was called to. This shifted my whole paradigm of how I have and will approach money management in the future.

This biblical philosophy of not being a slave has paid off hugely. At the end of this month, I will have paid off close to 20K of house expenses and be well set up to tackle the new project and investments I've learned about. God has called me to wisdom and to really pay attention to how I give and how I take care of my everyday budgeting, which has brought such clarity in these last months with large expenses coming due. My management of this continues to bring life to me, and is something I am beginning to have pride in. I previously took no value in it and felt no accountability as a single man. I followed this class up with Wise Investor where the whole class was walked through how God wants me to think about my finances. To think about 100, 60, or 30-fold return instead of thinking, "I can lose this and be ok." I am now expecting God to do what he said, and to hear His heart on investing.

I had not wanted to chase money and still don't, but I received a biblical vision for it- that I would leave an inheritance for my children and my children's children. In that class, God showed me that he wanted me to give to the church and to the world, which is something I could get behind 100%. I see the future as an opportunity to bless my family and church by being in abundance and now I have hope for the future I didn't see one year ago. I know what God has started and is doing is big and I'm incredibly appreciative. One of the best things that happened is I saw how to help teach, build friendships, and grow in wisdom around finances in a family environment. I was blessed with 5 great friends I wouldn't have otherwise.

Josh Mellot, April 2021

I joined the Wise Money class because Holy Spirit told me to right after I had started going to The Summit Edmonton Church at the end of June 2019. Little did I know that my husband would separate from me literally the day before I started Wise Money on September 9.

Because I was new to The Summit Edmonton Church, I was wanting to find a Family Group, but Holy Spirit had not given me the go ahead with that which was so confusing considering I am such an extrovert. I will never forget on the first day of our Wise Money group, we were told that this was not only going to be 8 weeks of financial teachings but that we would now become a family. Of course, I started crying, because my Father in Heaven knew at that moment in my life, even before I did, that I would need a family.

I also needed teaching and support on how to be a good steward of my money for the tough road ahead as I was left with $27,000 of debt, a house that needed major renovations, a job loss, double the expenses with half the income, and doing all of this as a single mom. My goal was to be debt free by March 31, 2021, which was a hefty goal considering the circumstances, but I serve a Big God who told me that He alone would be my provider and I chose to trust Him. But here's the best part.... on March 12, 2021, I became debt FREE! Thank you to everyone for loving on me, supporting me, and praying for me during a rough season that was also a wonderful season to grow in my full reliance and trust on God. He is so good all the time.

Dana Goodwin, March 2021

The Wise Money course helped us understand our finances from a biblical lens. The teaching helped us to understand the "behind the scenes" of how the credit card/financing industry works which solidified our decision to steer away from ever borrowing money again. We made some poor financial decisions when we were first married 5 years ago. Today we are halfway to paying off our total debt including mortgage! Wise Money helped us to have fun with the process. Each week, I look forward to paying down our debt and I have learned the significance of living below our means; delayed gratification vs instant gratification. Praise God for teaching us how to live financially free while we are young.

Devon and Layla Edwards, April 2021

Testimonies About Business

We have been designing an app for a few years now. There has been seemingly a lot of 'delay' which at times has been discouraging, leaving us wondering what it would become, and if it was worth all the risk. Over the course of this waiting, God has shown that He is faithful many times and that He was with us in this endeavour.

We had been working with our marketing team on all the behind the scenes work on the website and preparing for the release. We needed to film a few scenes and needed some actors. We were going to use whoever volunteered, but there was a woman who inquired who was an Instagram influencer who had a following of about 9 000 people. Because of the nature of this business (an app, which is pregnancy/mom related) a 'Mom influencer' would have been an amazing way to give our app exposure, so this was super exciting. Unfortunately, when I clicked on her page it was clear that her main thing was yoga. I thought for a moment that maybe we could still use her and film something else, but the Holy Spirit nudged me and was like "Morgan, do you really want your app to be promoting this?" I didn't, so I had to decline her offer.

The next day I received an email with the models who had been chosen and at the bottom of the page there was a woman who also was a 'Mom influencer', with over 125 000 people, over ten times the amount of the other influencer! We filmed the scenes, and it was amazing. She already posted about the app on her page and would do so again when the app is released. This is free exposure to the perfect audience. I couldn't have arranged this if I tried. I really felt this was a moment that God was showing me that integrity is absolutely essential in Kingdom Business, and when you decline opportunities that seem good for business but conflict with your convictions, that He is preparing your heart to open an even bigger door. It's showed me that He's been with us in this process, and to trust Him knowing that He will open all the doors and set up every divine connection we need to get things done.

Morgan Sutherland, May 2021

Testimonies About Having Children

In December 2020, I found out I was pregnant. Everything seemed fine and normal, with no concerns. In March of 2021, I had an ultrasound where they found a cyst on the baby's brain. Based on the cyst, it was an indication of Trisomy 18. Trisomy 18 basically means your baby will die in childbirth or shortly after childbirth. I then went for a specialized blood test that would give them a better idea of whether the baby had Trisomy 18 or didn't. The blood test came back showing an even higher chance of having Trisomy 18. From there I met with a geneticist at the Royal Alex Hospital. They advised me of another blood test through the United States that I could pay to have done that would give me either a high percentage or low percentage result. I could have that test or an amniocentesis. We opted for the one out of the US first as an amniocentesis can be damaging in itself.

While awaiting the results from California, I received prayer during our bi-weekly women's group at our church, The Summit Edmonton. The Lord told me to put my faith in Him and lay down my worries, as I was living in constant fear that my baby would not live past birth. About a week later we received the results. Our baby was low risk for having Trisomy 18. We continued with the rest of the pregnancy thanking the Lord for his goodness. Our baby, Trace, is now 4 months old and healthy as can be.

Kristy Kingsley, Dec 2021

Our testimony is a testimony of family. We've been married 17 years now and the last few years have been unbelievable to see God work in growing our family when we thought it was impossible.

With male factor infertility, we waited on God for several years early on in our marriage, not knowing how we would grow our family. Through the miracle of adoption, we brought home our Jamaican son after a 7-year adoption journey.

The miracle of our next son through embryo adoption is something I love to talk about. I love adoption as it is, but embryo adoption is something not many know about. And though embryo adoption is not technically like traditional adoption (it happens through donated embryos), to us, it is just as much a miracle.

The way it works is families who have undergone IVF and have remaining embryos frozen in fertility clinics can choose to donate them to families who want to have a baby that otherwise can't. I hadn't known of this option myself until a couple years ago.

I always wanted to experience pregnancy and birth. So, as we felt the Lord leading us in this direction and it became a reality for me, it was such a redeeming experience that I truly loved every moment of. I had a wonderful pregnancy, not perfect, but nothing could take my joy away no matter what symptom. God gave me one of my greatest heart's desires. Feeling our baby growing and moving inside me was a miraculous feeling day by day and we couldn't wait to meet the little one growing inside of me. I was so in awe of what God had done for us and I would lay there, so intent on feeling the baby that I even felt movement earlier than they say you should! Just miraculous.

We have a beautiful relationship with our son's genetic family who donated their embryos to us. They had our son's embryo frozen for 15 years. The way God worked in this beautiful relationship is so special to us. They've become family. Family isn't always blood, and we are so in awe the way God has grown our family when we thought it impossible.

Kassian was born in October 2021 and is a miraculous addition to our family.

Rita Green, October 2021

Testimonies About Children

During this crazy time in the world, we have had the blessed opportunity to see our 5-year-old son Israel begin to have his own relationship with the Lord. It has been such a beautiful experience.

When I was pregnant, I prayed that like John, Israel too would be filled with the Holy Spirit in my womb. Now that Israel is five, his prayers totally leave us in awe. At first, we heard him praying in tongues, then we heard him pray that God would begin to raise people from the dead. He began to call out the names of his cousins asking God that they would receive more Holy Spirit; more and more and more. Then it became more generalized, praying for the nations. We have asked him a couple of times to pray for healing for us, and we have seen God using him in this way. We know that Israel will live up to his name and be triumphant with God. We know that with faith like this, we will see God using Israel to bring about many miracles, bringing us into this new season of glory in the kingdom of God. Hallelujah, thank you Jesus!

Angel Sanders, June 2021

We were watching the livestream church service at home and my four-year-old son started praying in tongues!

Amber, November 2021

Testimonies From the Youth BLEND

I have been at Summit for 2 years now, but before that, I was at my old church for about 14-15 years, which was my whole life. When we first moved churches, I was terrified because my old church was all I had ever known, and they were all the friends that I had. When my parents told me they prayed about it and that God told them it was time to move on to attend Summit, I didn't know what to say. I didn't understand why God wanted us to move.

On the first night of the Youth BLEND in August 2021, all of us youth were sitting by the campfire singing songs, talking, eating marshmallows, and having hot chocolate. It finally dawned on me what Summit has done for me in the past 2 years. I met new friends and reunited with old friends. I have never felt more at home than this church makes me feel. I realized how much I have depended on church and especially the Youth Group this year more than ever. This year I have struggled with the loss of hope, depression, and mental meltdowns, and someone that I know and loved committed suicide. But during the BLEND retreat, I felt God say that this is the reason that He brought me here, because this church has been my rock, and I don't know where I would be without it. Jesus knew that this year and a half would be difficult, and he knew that this church, which is my second family, would help me through it. Also, for that past little while, my neck has been really sore and bothering me, and during the service on Friday evening it stopped!

Sophie Bayne, August 2021

At the Youth BLEND camp one afternoon, a leader got tipped off his paddle board and lost his glasses in the lake. A bunch of people along with himself looked, but no one could find them. The male leader needed them to see out of one eye, so it was vital to find them.

At dinner, another Youth Leader felt that instead of doing pre-service prayer in the chapel that we should meet at the lake to pray for the glasses to be resurrected. The students gathered full of faith, as they'd already witnessed so many miracles that week. They came in swimsuits, prayed, and went in the water looking. After half an hour, there was still no sign of the glasses. The excitement and faith started to disperse, so the students went and got ready for the evening service despite not finding the glasses. They went after the Lord in worship, knowing it was a pretty big impossibility that the glasses would be found.

The male counsellor knew what the Lord had said to him, "Go pray and believe for the glasses!" After an hour of searching, someone said, "Feel with your hands." He felt nothing, but a few minutes later he went back to that same spot in faith. They were just talking and praying in the water. The counsellor was moving his hands as he prayed and he felt seaweed, and sure enough, the glasses were tangled in it!

Halfway through worship, the kids were in an intimate place of worship, and the counsellor showed up completely soaked, but with the glasses on his face! I'm telling you when he and the other leaders came in with the glasses on, the cap came off the students. Celebration and weeping flooded across the altar as they witnessed this crazy miracle! Literally the wonder and awe of God filled the room.

Anonymous, August 2021

Testimonies About Safety

Early Saturday morning, I saw a Kijiji ad for some equipment that I was looking to add for our business from a seller in remote Northern Saskatchewan. The equipment I require is quite technical and takes 6 months for delivery from China, so I was pretty excited to see an ad for some similar equipment that was only a 7-hour drive. I sent the seller an email through Kijiji and told him I would be there for noon with cash in hand. I grabbed $5,000 in cash and left for Northern Saskatchewan. I was hoping this small community was a nice Mennonite community but once I arrived, I realized it was a different type of community and I could feel the oppression when I arrived. I told myself, "Lets get this deal done and get out of Dodge as fast as I can." This place was so remote, the last 45 minutes of the drive was on about 90 KMs of gravel with a posted speed limit of 80 km/hr and no cell coverage or internet.

The seller was emailing me while I was driving, asking me to pay him a $2,000 deposit with Crypto currency which I wasn't willing to do until I met him and saw the equipment. I told him I'll give him a 100% deposit in cash and for us to meet. He

86

wouldn't give me his address until I sent him the Crypto so I told him where I was located and that we could meet at the local store so someone could witness the sale if he wanted. He then emailed me that he was testing me to make sure I was actually here. That's when I knew he was setting me up to rob me or worse.

Right then I heard Holy Spirit tell me "Leave Now!" He didn't have to tell me twice. I took off out of there, gravel and dust flying behind me. Through a break in the dust behind me, I saw head lights in my mirror, so I brought my speed up to 120 km/hr, but I noticed a truck was closing on me, so I started driving like Jehu at 140 km/hr to keep them in my mirror. My heart was racing, and I was getting scared, because who drives that fast on a bad gravel road? Then some really negative thoughts started to overtake me. Thoughts of a what a violent death might be like out here and that my wife may never know what even happened to me.

I tried to get 911 on autodial so that if what I thought might happen, at least my wife might know my last known location. They connected for about 5 seconds and then I lost them due to bad service. It was pretty scary to say the least. Then I saw a truck coming towards me and as I went screaming by him at 140 km/hr, I noticed it was RCMP, but they didn't stop. It was like they didn't even see me. I could still see this truck behind me, so I sped up to 160 km/hr and said, "OK Jesus." That's when one of the songs we sing at Summit came into my head, "It may seem like I'm surrounded, but I'm surrounded by You... This is how I fight my battles, this how I fight my battles...." That's when I remembered to worship before the battle. I grabbed my phone and put on some worship music, and as Pastor Nikki started singing and I started praying in tongues something changed.

The terrifying fear that I was experiencing turned into battle confidence. I was still frightened but ready to fight at the wheel because my God fights my battles. As I was praising Jesus and claiming His promises over my life, that no weapon formed against me will prosper and decreeing that I stop any assignment of the enemy against me in the name of Jesus Christ, I looked back in the mirror and all I saw was dust flying behind me now. The truck was gone. That's when I realized that there must be the Lord's angel sitting on my fenders to have kept my car out of the ditch at those speeds.

I wasn't even fishtailing around the corners at 140 km/hr. It was like I was on a track.

As I was speeding down the gravel road, I sensed what I now know to be touching the Kingdom of our God here on Earth as I felt as if my entire car was in a vacuum moving through space and time down the road uninhibited by the natural laws of physics that would have normally made it impossible to handle and control the vehicle on gravel at that speed.

Wow what a miracle! Thank you, Jesus!

Aaron Ursulak, September 2021

Testimonies About Miracles

I had some old friends 25 years ago, Perry and Jackie, that because of my lifestyle of being in the occult, had to cut me out of their life. Recently I was thinking about them, because I have gotten saved and have left all my occultic practices. I was thinking it would be good to reconnect with them. I looked them up and found their phone number. I called and left a message and didn't hear anything back. A couple weeks went by, and I heard God say to go to Safeway even though I didn't need anything from Safeway. I got there and asked Him, "Now what?" I heard Him say to go to the meat counter.

When I went to the meat counter, I saw a man, wearing his mask, and he looked familiar. I walked over and I touched his arm. I said," Are you Perry?" And he's like, "Yes I am." I said, "I'm Tracey." He recognized me, and said, "Oh, Jackie got your message. She's really bad at phoning people back. Come on over." So, after 25 years, God reconnected me with the Christians from my past who loved me and tried to show me the Lord.

Tracey Gusta, May 2021

At the Builders Collab Christmas Market, I won a gift basket. You have no idea what this gift basket meant to me. I don't get any Christmas presents under the tree. God is revealing himself to me as my husband this last couple of weeks. And this gift basket was like a gift from Him!

I've also been given a few prophetic words publicly, and I went to God saying I feel like I'm being a little greedy, I'm coming to expect from You, and I sensed Him say it is My will for you to be loved upon.

So I felt a little sheepishly silly. I was content with the words He had given me, the little gifts like toilet paper on sale, the parking space at the front, things like that, I was just really thankful for everything that came my way recognizing it is a gift from Him. And then I received the text that I won this gift basket. Everything is willed by Him.

My husband, the Lord, wanted me to receive this gift. I had no idea what was in it. I actually even declined filling out a ballot at first, feeling a little greedy. My first thought was there was somebody who absolutely deserved the basket, and I hoped the right person won. I was encouraged again to fill one out, so I did, and then to find out I won?

I was fearful this was going to be the leanest Christmas ever. I wasn't working, I had absolutely no income coming in at all. I was a little stressed out, OK, a lot stressed out. But there is a sense of peace here that I have never experienced. I know that my husband, the Lord, is taking care of us, I just have to trust Him.

This gift basket was a gift from the Lord, and it helped me to see Him as my husband, and to know that He is taking care of me, no matter the circumstances.

Then, on Christmas Eve, my employer contacted me, and they accepted my medical claim, and I will get back pay from September onward, plus all medication reimbursements! God is such an incredible provider.

Candace Blatchford, December 2021

Testimonies About Deliverance

I started smoking cigarettes when I turned 16, Sportmans regular. My father bought them for my 16th birthday. There was not the information about cigarettes as there is today. Even doctors said there was no harm in smoking. I smoked to be cool and grown up with no worry about my health.

Over 21 years later when I was 46 years old, I wanted to quit smoking. I became a Christian and didn't want to indulge in that addiction. I tried to use my will power and failed many, many times. I tried hypnosis which worked for a little while. I also asked the Lord to relieve me of this addiction and He did. However, I picked it up again and struggled for a few more years.

I read books on quitting smoking, and it worked for a year. I fell back into my addiction when I went hunting with a smoking friend. Then vapes came out so I started using them, nice flavors and lots to try. I used them for 6 months then went back to cigarettes.

Over and over again, I tried to quit and failed. One night when I was laying in bed, very upset that I was still smoking, I said to God "Please help. I'm so very tired of this addiction." I was extremely mad and not at all humble in prayer. "I am angry, can you help Lord?"

Then next morning, I had no urge to smoke. I usually woke up and the first thing I did was smoke. But this time, I did not even want to smoke. I wasn't craving it at all!

It's been only 5 months and I don't have a single urge to smoke. I even went hunting with a smoking friend and I did not want to indulge.

Jesus worked out what I could not do better than I could ever do.

Terry Beaver, December 2021

The Summit Edmonton Church

In 2009, Chris and Nikki Mathis planted Fresh Anointing House of Worship in Crestview, Florida, USA. In 2013, the organization name was changed to The Summit. It began to expand and consisted of other churches and ministries being planted as well as many becoming affiliated with this church.

In 2017, Pastors Chris and Nikki took three churches, River City Church of Edmonton, Fresh Oil & Fire Apostolic Church, and Revival Family Gathering, that were all under Summit Global and merged them to become The Summit Edmonton Church in Edmonton, Alberta, Canada.

Chris and Nikki felt called to come to Canada to pastorally lead this church. It has grown substantially since then, and as of 2020, it has grown to have both an East and West location in Edmonton.

Chris and Nikki, through their partner ministry, Summit Global Ministries- Edmonton, oversee churches across Canada, the USA, and Brazil, as well as The Summit Edmonton Church. They continue to have a heart for church planting, and they look forward to seeing revival stretch across the world.

The core values of The Summit Edmonton Church are Family, Devotion, Revival and Hope.

Find us at www.thesummitchurch.ca

Other Books by
Summit Global Publishing Ltd.

Living in Devotion

A 40-day devotional book by
The Summit Edmonton
Church

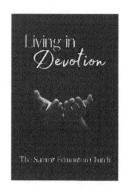

Hope for the Broken Soul

by Louise Franck

Summit Global Publishing Ltd.

In December 2020, Tracy Belford received a vision from the Lord to open a publishing company. The purpose was to share the word of the Lord that was coming out of The Summit Edmonton Church. She was inspired by Romans 10:17 (NKJV) *"So then faith comes by hearing, and hearing by the word of God."*

Tracy believed that God was sharing so much wisdom and revelation within her church that it needed to be shared on a larger scale to increase the faith of many. To date, she has published two books: Living in Devotion, a collaboration of The Summit Edmonton Church leadership, and Hope for the Broken by Louise Franck.

Upcoming books include:

- Revival Paradigm

- Signs, Wonders and Miracles- Testimonies from The Summit Vol 2

Summit Global Publishing Ltd. continues to accept manuscripts from individuals within the Summit Global family. To submit a manuscript, please email tracy@thesummitchurch.ca

Manufactured by Amazon.ca
Bolton, ON

33198733R00057